Contents

Stealth Battles

Not all battles are fought with huge armies or war machines. The most important struggles are often behind the scenes.

Palpatine, with his true identity as Darth Sidious, is a master of stealth. He wins battles by manipulating people, often without them even noticing! His rise to power, the creation of his army, and persuading Anakin Skywalker to join the dark side are all achieved by twisting the will of others to fulfil his own evil plans.

The light side uses stealth too, but for different, more honorable, reasons. The Jedi use the power of the Force to disguise their movements, so that they can carry out stealthy investigations. The rebels, fighting alongside the Jedi, learn to master the element of surprise and beat the Empire at its own game. Even a little astromech droid such as R2-D2 can be sent on a secret mission that, if successful, could be a major blow to Palpatine.

The Jedi Master Obi-Wan Kenobi goes on a secret mission after uncovering a plot against Senator Padmé Amidala. He must use his investigative skills to track down the attacker, but this only leads to more mysteries when a shadowy villain silences the attacker with a poison dart before she can say who sent her! And after learning that the dart comes from the planet Kamino, Obi-Wan uncovers even bigger surprises.

The people of Kamino have created a secret clone army. The clones are copies of the bounty hunter called Jango Fett. Obi-Wan suspects that Jango is behind the assassination attempt and so confronts him—only to discover that Jango's weapons are hard to beat. Jango soon escapes aboard his ship, *Slave I*.

Although Obi-Wan loses the fight against Jango, he has uncovered vital information. Thanks to the bounty hunter's Kaminoan dart, the Jedi now know about the secret army on Kamino—and can use it for themselves!

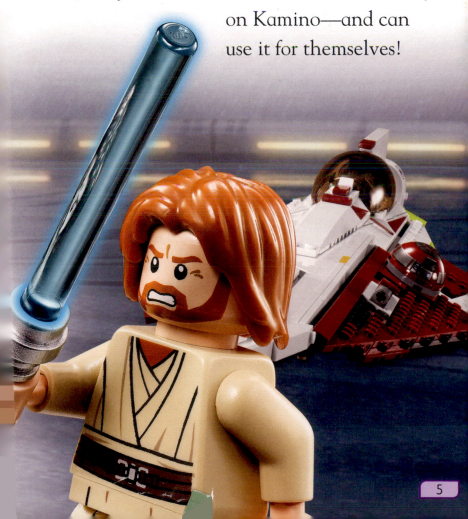

KNOW YOUR WARRIORS
BOUNTY HUNTERS

They hunt down people, and even Sith Lords use their services—they are bounty hunters. For the right price, they will even capture their friends.

BOBA
FETT

PHYSICAL ANALYSIS

"HE'S NO GOOD TO ME DEAD."
BOBA FETT

SPECIAL DEVICE
Rangefinders on helmets help bounty hunters track targets.

ARMOR
Boba's Mandalorian armor is made of tough durasteel.

WEAPON OF CHOICE

Bounty hunters go on missions fraught with dangers. Blaster guns are just what they need for self-protection or to get rid of an enemy.

75%
BATTLE SKILLS

▶ **KNOWN FOR** Stalking and catching

▶ **ALLEGIANCE** Anyone who can pay

▶ **PERSONALITY** Stealthy and clever

▶ **ENEMIES** Too many to count

▶ **STRENGTH** Quick reflexes

▶ **WEAKNESS** Can get overconfident

▶ **WATCH OUT FOR** Sudden strikes

• BATTLE STORY •

Han Solo has a bounty on his head. Greedo, a bounty hunter from Tatooine, finds him first. Han, however, proves too clever for Greedo. But Darth Vader outwits him and hands him over to Boba.

The Jedi should be suspicious of their new clone army, as the true hand behind its creation is Palpatine! The Sith Lord's rise to power, from senator to Chancellor—the most important job in the Republic—is through decades of clever, patient planning, and is the stealthiest work in all of the galaxy.

Palpatine engineers a war in the galaxy to weaken the Jedi and make people believe that they need a powerful Emperor to bring order to their worlds again. He then uses his clones to destroy the Jedi, thus eliminating his only threat.

Palpatine's biggest weapon is the angry, greedy Jedi Anakin Skywalker. Palpatine persuades Anakin to give in to his emotions and become the all-powerful Sith Lord Darth Vader. With his help, Palpatine achieves his ultimate goal of being made Emperor.

Yet stealthy Palpatine makes one big mistake! He does not know about Anakin's twin children, born in secret. One day they might be his undoing!

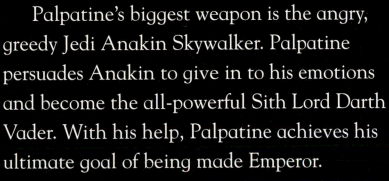

ORDER 66
HOW IT HAPPENED

Darth Sidious issued Order 66, a secret instruction to destroy all of the Jedi. Afterward, there was nobody left to challenge Sidious and he could make himself Emperor!

WHO DID WHAT?

Darth Sidious

This devious politician waited years to strike. With Order 66 he is finally rid of the Jedi.

Clone Troopers

The clone troopers received a secret message ordering them to destroy the Jedi that they were protecting.

Anakin Skywalker

Anakin secretly joined Sidious. He destroyed the Jedi Temple and all of the young Padawans, too.

On Kashyyyk, Jedi Grand Master Yoda battled Commander Gree. The experienced Jedi destroyed the clone officer and escaped.

Commander Cody almost destroyed Obi-Wan Kenobi on planet Utapau, but the Jedi Master managed a quick getaway.

MESSAGE OF HOPE

Obi-Wan Kenobi sent out a message warning any surviving Jedi to hide. The Empire will never stop looking for them.

"Our Jedi Order and the Republic have fallen—with the dark shadow of Empire rising to take their place."

"Do not return to the temple... that time has passed and our future is uncertain..."

In a galaxy full of important people like Emperor Palpatine, little astromech droids can pass by entirely unnoticed. The rebel Princess Leia is desperate, but also clever when she sends her droid R2-D2 on a top-secret mission.

Leia has learned about the Empire's Death Star. She has also managed to steal the plans! But she is in danger and needs to send a message to people who can stop the Empire. She knows of someone who can help—Obi-Wan Kenobi. He is hiding on Tatooine, so she sends R2-D2 to find him.

R2-D2 is brave and determined. It's not easy for a droid to wheel across Tatooine's sand, but he doesn't give up! Not even being captured by junk-collecting Jawas deters him from his mission. A bit of luck helps, too: his droid friend C-3PO persuades moisture farmer Owen Lars and his nephew, Luke Skywalker, to buy the pair of them from the Jawas. It is Luke who inadvertently leads R2-D2 to Obi-Wan, who has been watching from nearby. R2-D2 then reveals Leia's message, which he has been carefully hiding the whole time!

Not all secret missions go as planned. Sometimes the rebels' schemes go awry, and then they need quick thinking and teamwork to escape tricky situations.

When Luke Skywalker, Han Solo, and Chewbacca join Obi-Wan Kenobi's mission to rescue Princess Leia from the Death Star, the two humans plan to go undercover by disguising themselves as stormtoopers! The rescue is successful, but on the way back to Han's ship, the *Millennium Falcon*, they are forced to hide from some real stormtroopers in a trash compactor. When the compactor is suddenly turned on, they are nearly crushed. Thankfully they have back-up: C-3PO and R2-D2 are able to shut the compactor down.

The friends all meet back at the *Millennium Falcon* but watch helplessly as Darth Vader strikes down Obi-Wan Kenobi. They manage to escape because Obi-Wan distracted the Sith Lord for them. They know that Obi-Wan lost this battle to help them get away.

IMPERIAL FLEET

IT'S A COLORFUL galaxy out there… and Darth Sidious doesn't like that one bit. That's why he builds his Empire's fleet in orderly shades of black, white, and lots of gray. It gives everything a nice, unified look, and it makes his ships so much easier to keep clean.

TIE ADVANCED
Darth Vader's prototype personal starfighter.
SIZE 30 feet (9.2 m) long
SPEED 105 MGLT
CAPACITY 1 pilot
WEAPONS 2 laser cannons, cluster missiles

TIE INTERCEPTOR
A faster and deadlier version of the TIE fighter.
SIZE 31.5 feet (9.6 m) long
SPEED 111 MGLT
CAPACITY 1 pilot
WEAPONS 4 laser cannons

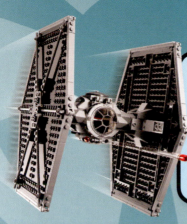

TIE FIGHTER
Standard twin ion engine combat starfighter.
SIZE 29.5 feet (8.99 m) long
SPEED 100 MGLT
CAPACITY 1 pilot
WEAPONS 2 laser cannons

TIE BOMBER
Slow but dangerous surface assault bomber.
SIZE 25.5 feet (7.8 m) long
SPEED 60 MGLT
CAPACITY 1 pilot
WEAPONS 2 laser cannons, 2 proton torpedo launchers

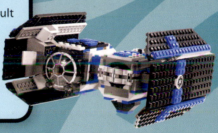

TIE DEFENDER
Experimental three-winged high-performance starfighter.
SIZE 30 feet (9.2 m) long
SPEED 144 MGLT
CAPACITY 1 pilot
WEAPONS 4 laser cannons, 2 ion cannons, 2 warhead launchers

Mind Wars

It doesn't matter how many planets you conquer or how big your army is—no war is ever really over until you win the battle of the mind. The evil Sith are experts at this kind of warfare. They use trickery and lies to make people think differently. The Jedi have mind tricks of their own, but they use them with care not to do any harm. In fact, mind wars can be found everywhere in the galaxy. Even Padmé Amidala convincing the Gungans to join her fight against an army of droids is a battle to decide the best thing to do.

Some mind wars are very brief, as when Darth Vader uses threats to make Princess Leia tell him where the rebels are hiding (he fails). Others last for years, as when Darth Sidious slowly lures Anakin Skywalker over to the dark side (he succeeds). The scary thing is, you might not even know when a mind war is happening!

FACE OFF
Jedi Master vs Sith Lord

Palpatine's secret is out. Mace Windu knows he is a Sith. But the Chancellor will not go down without a fight.

"You are under arrest, Chancellor!"

Mace Windu, Jedi Master

- **Strengths** Wise, master swordsman
- **Weakness** Too arrogant
- **Weapon** Purple lightsaber

When Anakin Skywalker turns to the dark side, it comes as a surprise to his Jedi friends. Master Yoda senses fear in him, but he does not know that Anakin's biggest fear is that something bad will happen to Padmé.

As a Sith Lord, Darth Sidious knows all about using people's fear against them. For years, he has tricked people into thinking he can protect them from problems that he has been secretly causing.

Sidious knows that Anakin is very worried about Padmé, so he tells him that the only way to protect her is to use the dark side of the Force.

Anakin does not want to join the dark side, but Sidious is a very convincing liar. He makes Anakin think that he has no choice! So Anakin joins forces with Darth Sidious and helps him to defeat Jedi Master Mace Windu.

There is no way back for Anakin now. His fear has become anger. Perhaps he could have defeated Darth Sidious in a lightsaber battle, but instead he has been beaten with clever words. He has turned his back on the Jedi and become a Sith!

When Anakin Skywalker turns to the
dark side, he takes a new name: Darth
Vader! It is exactly what Darth Sidious
wanted. Now nothing can stop them from
creating an Empire to rule the galaxy!

One of the planets in this new Empire
is Lothal. The people who live there don't
like Darth Sidious or Darth Vader, and
a group of rebels does its best to make life
hard for their evil rulers.

The Empire must fight a constant battle
to keep the people under control, so every

year they hold an event called Empire Day. This grand military parade of stormtroopers and AT-DP walkers looks like a celebration, but it is really meant to show everyone just how powerful the Empire is. It is a kind of mind war called propaganda. Over time, it is designed to change the way people think!

The rebels of Lothal know that the best way to fight the Empire's propaganda is with a clear message of their own. So they attack the parade to make it look weak, and write messages of resistance wherever they go.

POWERS OF THE DARK SIDE

THE DARK SIDE promises immense knowledge and strength to those who study the ways of the Sith. It also offers special powers, many of which are forbidden to the Jedi. Here are some of the strange and dangerous abilities that Sith Lords can call upon to frighten their followers and vanquish their foes.

YIKES! IT'S GETTING A LITTLE WINDY IN HERE!

TELEKINESIS

One of Darth Vader's mightiest talents is the ability to lift objects without touching them, and then throw them through the air at his opponents. Vader uses this power against Luke Skywalker on Cloud City, battering the unsuspecting rebel with metal wreckage and smashing the large protective window behind him.

FORCE LIGHTNING

By channeling dark side energy through his body, a Sith Lord like Darth Sidious can hurl crackling electricity from his bare hands to punish or destroy those who anger him. Only a great Jedi can hope to resist this shocking power.

YOU'D BETTER BE.

ACK! S-SORRY I F-FORGOT YOUR BIRTHDAY, LORD VADER!

FORCE CHOKE

A common penalty for failing or displeasing Vader is the Force choke, which even works across large distances. A fortunate victim may be released if the Sith Lord is feeling merciful. As for the less fortunate ones… well, there are always more Imperial officers looking for a promotion.

Even the Jedi play mind games from time to time! Unlike the Sith, they are careful not to abuse their powers—but a Jedi mind trick can be very useful for getting out of a sticky situation without using a lightsaber!

On Tatooine, Obi-Wan Kenobi, C-3PO, and Luke Skywalker are on a mission to smuggle R2-D2 to the Rebel Alliance when they are stopped by two sandtroopers. These special stormtroopers have been warned to watch out for droids, and there's no hiding R2-D2 and C-3PO! Luckily, the sandtroopers are not very strong-minded and Obi-Wan is able to plant a suggestion in their minds using the Force. "These are not the droids you're looking for," he tells them with a wave of his hand. "These are not the droids we're looking for," they agree!

Things aren't so easy when Obi-Wan tries to use his mind tricks on an angry customer in the Mos Eisley Cantina—his mind is too strong with rage. That's when having a lightsaber also comes in handy!

KNOW YOUR WARRIORS
SITH

The Force is strong in the Sith and they use it to destroy all of those who defy them. They lurk in the shadows making sneaky plans to take over the galaxy.

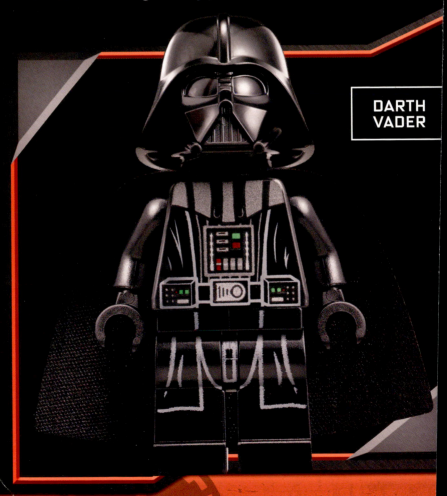

DARTH VADER

PHYSICAL ANALYSIS

"DON'T MAKE ME DESTROY YOU!"
DARTH VADER

VADER'S MASK
Filter helps with breathing and also makes a scary sound.

SPECIAL SUIT
Complex mesh of wires and buttons keeps Vader alive.

WEAPON OF CHOICE

Beware a Sith wielding a red-bladed lightsaber. Darth Vader can swing his with fierce speed, and Darth Maul's has two blades for double the trouble!

95%
BATTLE SKILLS

▶ **KNOWN FOR** Unjust rule

▶ **ALLEGIANCE** To themselves

▶ **PERSONALITY** Evil, cunning

▶ **ENEMIES** Jedi, Rebel Alliance

▶ **STRENGTH** Imperial army, the Force

▶ **WEAKNESS** Greed for power

▶ **WATCH OUT FOR** Force choke

• BATTLE STORY •
Sith Lord Darth Vader shows no mercy—even to those on his own side. When the Imperial officer Admiral Ozzel allows the rebels to escape in the Battle of Hoth, he is never heard from again!

Darth Sidious was very pleased with himself when he lured Anakin Skywalker to the dark side and turned him into Darth Vader. So it's no surprise when he tries to do the same thing with Anakin's son, Luke!

The sneaky Sith uses lots of different mind tricks to convince Luke to join him. First, he tries to make Luke lose hope by telling him that his friends are doomed. Then he makes Luke angry, in the hope that his rage will take him over. Finally, he manipulates Luke into fighting Vader, but Luke will not give in to his rage and destroy his father.

When Sidious sees that his plan is not working, he turns to violence—shooting Force lightning from his fingers at Luke! But Vader cannot stand by and see his son destroyed. So he picks up Darth Sidious and hurls him deep into the reactor core of the Death Star, never to be seen again!

Darth Sidious's devious mind war has succeeded in changing the mind of a Skywalker—it's just not the change he expected!

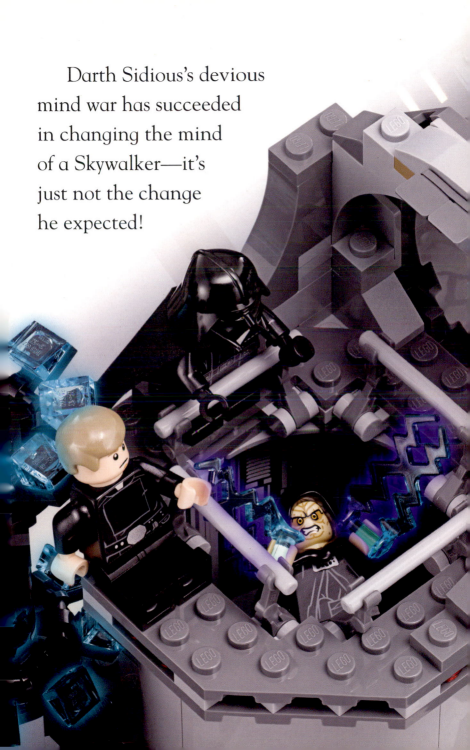

START

WOULD YOU USE THE FORCE FOR YOUR OWN GAIN?

YES

DO YOU ENJOY OBEYING A MASTER?

WHAT PATH WILL YOU TAKE?

NO

LIKE MANY OTHER SITH Lords, Anakin Skywalker started out a hero, but his choices led him down the path to the dark side. How would you end up if you faced the same choices he did? Answer the questions and discover your destiny!

YES

DO YOU BREAK THE RULES TO HELP YOUR FRIENDS?

YES

DO YOU SEEK REVENGE?

NO

NO

DO YOU ENJOY THE POWER OF BEING A JEDI KNIGHT?

NO

YES

YES →

SITH LORD
You have followed Darth Vader's terrible journey to the dark side and become a powerful Sith Lord. You rule by fear.

NO

WOULD YOU DO ANYTHING TO RULE THE GALAXY?

NO →

FALLEN JEDI
Like Pong Krell, you have been tempted by the dark side of the Force.

YES →

ARE YOU AFRAID OF FAILURE?

YES →

DARK SIDE WARRIOR
Just like Asajj, you are a bad guy, but you aren't a full Sith.

NO →

NO →

ROGUE
Jek-14 had to make the choice between dark and light. And so must you!

DO YOU OFTEN DO THE RIGHT THING?

YES →

JEDI KNIGHT
You have resisted the lure of the dark side and emerged a brave and noble hero—just like Luke Skywalker. Well done!

Nature's Dangers

Battles don't have to be between Sith and Jedi. Some of the toughest struggles are against something even Darth Sidious can't control: nature itself!

The sandstorms on the dry, desert planet of Tatooine, snow blizzards on icy Hoth, and the fiery lava of Mustafar can be just as menacing as an AT-AT. Worse still are some of the ferocious creatures that live across the galaxy—a cyborg wielding a lightsaber may not be as threatening as the bad-tempered rancor kept in Jabba the Hutt's dungeon, or a giant, hungry wampa on Hoth. And the thought of being swallowed by the terrifying Sarlacc on Tatooine is enough to scare even the meanest bounty hunter.

Survival often means learning to work with nature, rather than against it. In the maze-like forests of Endor, the rebels must quickly learn how to work with the furry Ewoks, or risk being eaten in a sacrificial ceremony! And when Obi-Wan Kenobi battles Anakin Skywalker on Mustafar, he must dodge blows from his former apprentice at the same time as trying not to fall into the scorching-hot lava beneath them.

When the rebels pick Hoth as a base to hide from the Empire, they don't choose it for its climate! The icy temperatures are cold enough to freeze rebels, so they must wrap up warm. In order to check the surroundings for any signs of spies from the Empire, the rebels ride smelly but harmless creatures called tauntauns, who have wide feet for trekking through Hoth's deep snowdrifts. But, as Luke Skywalker discovers, there are bigger dangers than snow and ice around!

Tauntauns are the favorite snack of another creature well-adapted to the cold of Hoth: the wampa. Luke must fight for his life when he and his tauntaun are snatched by the huge, clawed paws of one of these hungry beasts. The wampa begins to eat the tauntaun, but keeps Luke hanging upside down in his cave as an ice-cold dessert for later!

Using the Force, Luke manages to grab his lightsaber. With one swing he injures the monster and makes a quick escape. Phew!

Quiz

1. On which planet is the clone army created?

2. What is the name of Darth Sidious's instruction to destroy all of the Jedi?

3. Where does Princess Leia send R2-D2 to look for Obi-Wan Kenobi?

4. What color is Mace Windu's lightsaber?

5. What kind of farmer is Owen Lars?

6. How do Luke Skywalker and Han Solo disguise themselves to rescue Princess Leia?

7. What creature do wampas like to eat?

8. Which bad-tempered creature is kept in Jabba the Hutt's dungeon?

9. How often is Empire Day held?

10. Where is Darth Sidious finally defeated?

See page 42 for answers

Glossary

Awry
Gone wrong, not according to plan.

Bounty hunter
Someone who hunts down other people for a reward, often money.

Chancellor
Important and powerful politician.

Clone
Identical copy of another person or object.

Cyborg
Living being whose body is made up of some robotic parts.

Droid
Metal robot.

Empire
Group of worlds ruled over by one leader, called an Emperor.

Galaxy
Group of millions of stars and planets.

Quiz answers:
1. Kamino 2. Order 66
3. Tatooine 4. Purple
5. He is a moisture farmer 6. They dress up as stormtroopers
7. Tauntauns 8. The rancor 9. Every year
10. The Death Star